*Nita Mehta's*

# Taste of Delhi

**Vegetarian**

## 100% TRIED & TESTED RECIPES

*Nita Mehta*

B.Sc. (Home Science), M.Sc. (Food and Nutrition) Gold Medalist

*Tanya Mehta*

**SNAB**
PUBLISHERS PVT LTD

*Nita Mehta's*
# Taste of Delhi

© Copyright 2004  **SNAB** Publishers Pvt Ltd

First Edition 2004
ISBN 81-7869-080-2

*Food Styling and Photography:* **SNAB**

*Layout and laser typesetting :*

 National Information Technology Academy
3A/3, Asaf Ali Road
New Delhi-110002
☎ 23252948

*Distributed by :*
THE VARIETY BOOK DEPOT
A.V.G. Bhavan, M 3 Con Circus,
New Delhi - 110 001
Tel : 23417175, 23412567; Fax : 23415335
Email: varietybookdepot@rediffmail.com

*Published by :*

**SNAB**
**Publishers Pvt. Ltd.**
3A/3 Asaf Ali Road,
New Delhi - 110002
Tel: 23252948, 23250091
Telefax:91-11-23250091

*Editorial and Marketing office:*
**E-159, Greater Kailash-II, N.Delhi-48**
*Fax:* 91-11-29225218, 29229558
*Tel:* 91-11-29214011, 29218727, 29218574
*E-Mail:* nitamehta@email.com
snab@snabindia.com
*Website:*http://www.nitamehta.com
*Website:* http://www.snabindia.com

*Printed by :*
THOMSON PRESS (INDIA) LIMITED

**Rs. 89/-**

# Introduction

What exactly is Delhi food? To find out, we took a walk around the old city and got the feel of the food eaten in *Purani Dilli*. The food was rich and varied. Delhi has such a variety and combination of rich *Punjabi, Mughlai* food, tasty vegetarian food of *Uttar Pradesh*. Roaming around the streets of *Chandni Chowk*, the *Jama Masjid* areas and *Daryaganj* we throughly enjoyed the street food. I spoke to food-stall owners, the expert cooks in their own specialties, asked them to share their secrets of masalas and other cooking ingredients. We tried out all the recipes and I have penned down these to give you the real, authentic Delhi food!

The book starts with a section on **Chaats** which is followed by Nashta or Snacks. The extremely soft dahi badas of *Chandni Chowk*, with just the right crispness and the delicious fruit kulle are difficult to get anywhere else. What better brunch than the **Bervi Poori with Aloo ki Subzi** from the famous Kedarnath Premchand Halwai of Chandni Chowk. Finally, we have the *khaas meetha* of Dariba. All recipes are modified and made simple to cook and serve, retaining the authenticity of the food.

*Nita Mehta*

## ABOUT THE RECIPES

### WHAT'S IN A CUP?

**INDIAN CUP**
1 teacup = 200 ml liquid
**AMERICAN CUP**
1 cup = 240 ml liquid (8 oz.)
**The recipes in this book were tested with the Indian teacup which holds 200 ml liquid.**

# CONTENTS

## Purani Dilli ke Nashte aur Snacks

## Dilli Walon ki Subziyan   48

# Chandni Chowk Ki
## CHAAT

# Masala Kaju

*It is important to fry cashews carefully as they turn brown very fast. Keep stirring all the time while frying, till they change colour, for about a minute. Shut off the flame and start removing them from oil. Do not wait till all of them turn golden.*

*Serves 4-5*

**1 cup (100 gm) cashewnuts (kaju)**
**¾ tsp black pepper powder, preferably freshly ground, ¼ tsp amchoor**
**1½ tsp chat masala, ¼ tsp garam masala, ¼ tsp red chilli powder**

1. Mix all the masalas together and keep ready. Heat 2 cups oil for frying. Reduce heat. Add kajus and stir fry continuously till they start changing colour and turn light golden. Shut off the flame. Remove from oil in a big bowl.
2. Immediately sprinkle the masalas while the kajus are still hot. Mix thoroughly with the fingers. Mix again after 2-3 minutes. Let it cool down.
3. When cool, store in air tight container. Serve with drinks.

# Ram Laddoo

## Topped with Mooli & Hari Chutney

*A very common street food in the lanes of old Delhi. While roaming in chandini chowk, I once happened to ask a hawker selling these laddos. "How do you make your laddoos so light and fluffy?" I was rather upset with his reply. "You know memsahib (madam), my arm and shoulder start paining when I beat the pithi (ground dal) for more than 30 minutes everyday"*

*At that moment I actually felt like gifting him an electric hand mixer to make his job simpler. Thanks to the modern machines. The same lightness can now be achieved by beating the ground dal with an electric mixture for about 5-7 minutes and without giving us any aches and pains!*

*Picture on cover*                    *Serves 5-6*

**½ cup (200 gm) dhuli mung ki dal (husked green beans)**
**½ cup channe ki dal, ½ tsp salt, oil for deep frying**

**ACCOMPANIMENTS**
**1 mooli (white radish) - peeled and grated**
**some hari chutney, see page 101**

1. Wash both the dals and soak together in some water overnight.
2. Next day strain dals. Grind them together to a **rough** paste in a mixer grinder, using very little water, only if required. Do not make it into a smooth paste.
3. Beat ground dal in a bowl with an electric hand mixer for 5-7 minutes till it feels really light and frothy of a soft dropping consistency, like that of a cake batter. Add salt. Mix well. To check it it is done put a small ball of beaten dal paste in a bowl of water. If it rises to the surface, it is done, otherwise beat some more.
4. Heat oil in a kadhai for deep frying. To test if oil is hot enough, drop a little paste into the kadhai. It should rise to the surface almost immediately.
5. Using wet fingers drop small amounts of paste into oil. Reduce heat to medium. When bubbles appear on the surface, turn and fry till golden yellow. Drain on paper napkins and serve topped with grated mooli and hari chutney.

# Fruit Kulle

*Hollowed cups of charcoal roasted potatoes are sold at Nai Sarak at the shop of Sultan. However, the potatoes can be boiled for a more practical version for the home kitchen. It started with potatoes and now kullas of all kinds of fruits and vegetables have become popular.*

*Picture on page 2*                 *Serves 6*

**3 small potatoes - boiled , 3 small tomatoes**
**1 kheera - peeled and cut into 6 pieces, about 1½" long**

**FILLING**
**½ cup channas (safeed chhole) - soak in warm water for 1 hour**
**½ cup fresh anaar ke dane (pomegranate kernels)**
**½ cup grapes (use black or green) - each cut into half from the middle**
**½ cup peas (matar)- boiled**
**2-3 green chillies - deseeded and chopped**
**1-2 tbsp chaat masala, preferably kala chat masala**
**½ tsp bhuna jeera (roasted cumin powder),**
**juice of ½ lemon, salt to taste**

1. Drain channas. Put them in a pressure cooker with 1 tsp salt and 1 cup water. Pressure cook to give 1 whistle. Remove from fire. Strain channas after pressure drops. Leave them in strainer (channi) for all the water to drain out.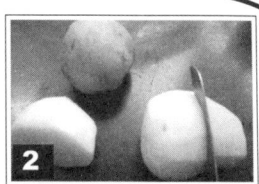

2. Peel the boiled potatoes. Cut each potato into 2 halves. Scoop out each piece with the help of a scooper or knife to get hollow cups. Sprinkle some lemon juice and chat masala in the potato cups and rub well. Keep aside.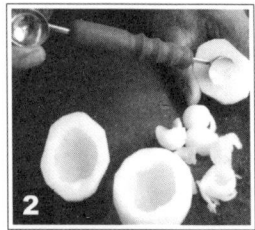

3. Cut the tomato into halves and scoop out the filling. Similarly scoop out the cucumber pieces with a knife or scooper, keeping the base intact. Sprinkle some lemon juice and chat masala in the cups.

4. For filling, mix all ingredients in a bowl. Check the filling and make it to your taste. Keep aside.

5. Fill each hollowed vegetable with this filling, heaping it a little. Serve.

# Aloo ki Tikki

*Picture on page 20*                    *Serves 8*

**5 medium (600 gm) potatoes - boiled and mashed**
**2 tbsp cornflour, 1 tsp salt, ½ tsp baking powder**
**5-6 tbsp ghee or oil for shallow frying**
**FILLING**
**½ cup dhuli moong dal (split, skinned green beans)**
**½ tsp jeera (cumin seed), 2 pinches hing (asafoetida)**
**½" piece ginger - finely chopped, 1 green chilli - finely chopped**
**1 tsp dhania powder, ½ tsp red chilli powder**
**½ tsp chaat masala, ½ tsp garam masala**
**1 tbsp coriander leaves - chopped,  ½ tsp salt**
**ACCOMPANIMENT- meethi imli chutney or saunth, see page 102**

1.  For the filling, soak dal overnight or for at least for 3-4 hours in water, keeping the water 2" above the dal. Drain dal and grind in a mixer to a rough paste. Do not grind too much, you should be able to see some whole dal grains in the dal paste. Grind for a few seconds only. Push

down the dal on the sides of the mixer with a spatula or knife and grind again for a few seconds to a rough paste.

2. For the filling, heat 3 tbsp oil or ghee in a kadhai. Add jeera and hing. Let jeera turn golden. Remove from fire. Add ginger, chopped green chilli, dhania powder, red chillies, chat masala and garam masala. Return to fire. Add coriander and dal paste. Add salt. Stir continuously for about 5 minutes on low medium heat. Do not dry it too much. Remove from fire and keep aside to cool.

3. Boil, peel and grate potatoes. Sprinkle 2 tbsp cornflour, 1 tsp salt and baking powder on potatoes. Mix nicely so that ingredients mix together.

4. Divide potato mixture into 8 portions. Take a ball of mashed potatoes. Make a shallow cup with ball of mashed potatoes. Place a tbsp full of dal filling in centre and seal well from all sides to cover the filling.

5. Heat oil on a non stick tawa or a frying pan. Shallow fry 2-3 tikkis at a time on low medium heat till golden and crisp on both sides. Once done, shift to the sides and put fresh ones in the centre. This way the tikkis turn really crisp. Serve hot topped with of imli ki meethi chutney.

# Matar Aur Kulche

*Picture on facing page*　　　　*Serves 4*

2 cups dry matar - soaked in water overnight
½ tsp jeera (cumin seeds), a pinch of hing (asafoetida), 1 tsp salt
1 tsp chaat masala powder, 1 tsp bhuna jeera powder (roasted cumin)
½ tsp garam masala powder, ½ tsp red chilli powder, ½ tsp amchoor

**JAL JEERA WATER(YOU CAN BUY READY MADE PACKET ALSO)**
½ of a small bunch poodina (25 gm)
a small lemon sized ball of seedless imli (tamarind) - washed well
1 tsp kala namak (black salt), ¾ tsp salt, 1 tsp jeera (cumin seeds)
5-6 tbsp saboot kali mirch (black peppercorns), ½ tsp saunf (fennel seeds)
½ tsp amchoor, a pinch of hing (asafoetida), 1 dry red chilli
seeds of 1 moti illaichi (black cardamom)

**TOPPING**
1 small onion - cut into ½, then slice widthwise to get half rings
½ of a firm tomato - cut into thin strips, ½" piece of ginger - cut into strips
1 green chilli - cut into half lengthwise, deseeded and finely chopped
juice of ½ lemon, or to taste

1. Drain water from soaked peas. Rub & wash again to discard any white skin. Put them in a pressure cooker. Add 1½ cups water. Pressure cook on high flame till two whistles and reduce flame and let it cook for 15 minutes. Remove from fire and let the pressure come down by itself.
2. Strain matars to discard any water. Remove any of those thin white skins. Leave them in strainer. Mash channas with the back of a karchi.
3. To prepare jal jeera water, grind all ingredients with 2 tbsp water to a paste. Remove to a bowl and add ½ cup water. Mix well and keep to rest for 3-4 hours. Strain through a muslin cloth (mal-mal ka kapda). (You can buy a ready made packet of jal jeera and make about ½ cup of it. Keep aside.)
4. To prepare the mattars, heat 2 tbsp oil in a kadhai. Add jeera. Remove from fire. Add hing, salt, chat masala, bhuna jeera, garam masala, red chilli powder and amchoor. Return to fire and stir for 30 seconds.
5. Add strained peas. Stir for 3-4 min. Add jal jeera and cook for 2 minutes. Mix well. Remove from fire and keep aside till serving time.
6. To serve, heat mattar. Transfer to a dish. Sprinkle onion, tomato, ginger & chilli. Squeeze lemon juice on it and mix lightly. Serve with kulchas.

◁ *Aloo Ki Tikki : Recipe on page 16*

# Dahi Bhalle

*Makes 25*

**1½ cups (250 gm) dhuli urad dal - washed**
**½" piece ginger - very finely chopped, 2-3 pinches of hing (asafoetida)**
**½ tsp salt, ½ tsp baking powder, 1 tsp jeera (cumin seeds), oil for frying**
**MIX TOGETHER**
**3 cups curds - beat well till smooth, 1 tsp powdered sugar**
**½ tsp red chilli powder, ¾ tsp salt**
**1 tsp bhuna jeera powder, ½ tsp kala namak**
**ACCOMPANIMENT - hari chutney and imli ki saunth, see page 101/102**

1. Wash & soak dal in enough water to cover the dal, for about 3 hours.
2. Strain dal. Grind in a mixer in 2 batches, with chopped ginger and hing to a rough paste. Do not over grind. Add about ¼ cup water if required to grind. Keep scraping the dal on the sides, of the mixer while grinding.
3. Transfer dal paste to a deep pan or patila. Add salt and baking powder.
4. Beat well for 5-7 minutes with an electric hand mixer till the mixture turns whitish and frothy. Add ¼ -½ cup hot water while beating, enough

to get a soft dropping consistency like that of a cake batter. Beat some more with the fingers to feel the mixture if it is light. To test if the mixture is ready, put a small drop of paste in a bowl of water. If it rises to the surface, it is done, otherwise beat some more.

5. Heat oil in a kadhai for deep frying. Wet the palm of your left hand. With wet hands, make bhalla with dal batter into 2" discs on the wet palm. Sprinkle some jeera seeds on it. Press lightly to stick the jeera and flatten the bhalla.

6. Deep fry 5-6 bhallas at a time in medium hot oil till they swell. Reduce heat to low and turn the side. Fry on low medium heat till light golden. Drain from oil, keep aside.

7. Beat curd. Add all the ingredients to the curd. Keep side.

8. Boil 6 cups water with 2 tsp salt. Remove from fire. Add bhallas. Soak in salted hot water for 5 minutes. Remove from water on to a plate.

9. After 5 minutes, press out water lightly. Dip in curd and arrange bhallas in a flat dish.

10. Pour the remaining curd on the arranged bhallas. Sprinkle imli chutney and hari chutney over it in circles. Garnish with red chilli powder, bhuna jeera powder and some roasted cashew bits (optional).

# Moong Chillah

*Lentil pancakes topped with onion, tomato and paneer, served folded into half and topped with hari chutney is a common sight at all Delhi food festivals. Make the pancakes slightly bigger and you can enjoy them as morning breakfast too.*

*Picture on inside front cover*     *Serves 6*

1 cup dhuli moong dal (split, skinned moong beans) - wash & soak
overnight
2 tbsp fresh curd (yogurt)
4 green chillies - cut into half lengthwise, deseeded and chopped
1 tbsp besan (gram flour), a big pinch of hing (asafoetida)
½ tsp baking powder
1 tsp salt, ¼ tsp haldi, ¼ tsp garam masala

**TOPPING**
1½ onions - very finely chopped
200 gm paneer - crumbled or roughly mashed
2-3 tbsp very finely chopped coriander
1 tsp salt, 1 tsp chat masala, ¼ tsp red chilli powder

1. Wash dal. Soak dal overnight or for at least 4-5 hours in some water till soft.
2. Drain away the water and grind to a smooth paste with curd and green chillies.
3. Remove to a big mixing bowl. Add all other ingredients of the pancake.
4. Beat well with an electric mixer till very light and fluffy, for about 3-4 minutes.
5. Add about ¼ cup water to the paste to get a fairly thick batter, of a very thick pouring consistency, like that of a dosa.
6. Mix all ingredients of the topping and keep aside.
7. Heat 1 tbsp oil in a non-stick tawa or pan. Remove from fire. Pour 2 tbsp of batter (about half kadcchi) and spread quickly in a circular outer motion (like a dosa) to a small, thin pancake of 4-5" diameter. Do not keep it thick.
8. Sprinkle some topping mixture on the chillah and press gently.
9. Pour some oil on the sides. Pour some oil on the top also. Turn side and let it turn crisp from both sides. Remove from fire.
10. Fold into half, serve hot with hari chutney.

# Shakarkandi Seekh ki Chat

*Serves 6-8*

**½ kg shakarkandi (sweet potatoes), (about 4 pieces)**
**8-10 kaju (cashewnuts) - chopped (2 tbsp)**
**2 tbsp khoya - crumbled (30 gm)**
**3 tbsp grated or mashed paneer (cottage cheese)**
**1 tsp finely chopped ginger**
**1 tbsp finely chopped poodina (mint leaves)**
**½ tsp garam masala powder, ½ tsp red chilli powder**
**¾ tsp black pepper powder (kali mirch), 1½ tsp salt**
**4 tbsp besan (gramflour)**
**TO SRRINKLE- 1 tsp chaat masala powder**

1. Put shakarkandi in a pressure cooker. Pour enough water to cover. Pressure cook to give 2 whistles and then keep on low heat for 3-4 minutes. Remove from fire and let the pressure drop. Peel and mash the sweet potatoes. Keep aside.

2. Heat 2-3 tbsp oil and fry the cahewnuts till golden. Remove from oil and keep aside.

3. Roast besan and kaju on a tawa for 2-3 minutes till fragrant.

4. Mix mashed sweet potatoes, khoya, paneer, ginger, poodina, garam masala powder, red chilli powder, kali mirch powder, salt and roasted besan and kaju.

5. Take a small ball of the mixture, Shape it like a 2" long seekh kebab.

6. Take a pencil or a skewer and push it carefully from one end of kebab to the other, without puncturing at any point.

7. Gently pull out skewer or the pencil. Keep the seekhs in the fridge for ½ hour.

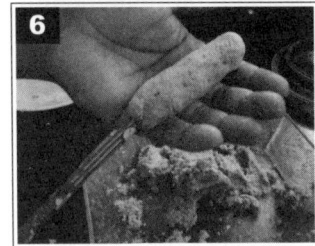

8. To serve, deep fry the seekhs in medium hot oil in a kadhai to a light brown colour. Sprinkle chaat masala and serve hot with poodina-dahi chutney .

# Gobhi Samosa

*Picture on page 76*                    *Serves 8-10*

**DOUGH**
**¾ cup plain flour (maida), ¼ cup fine semolina (suji)**
**¼ tsp salt, a pinch of baking powder**
**2 tbsp ghee or butter or margarine**

**VEGETABLE FILLING**
**1 medium cauliflower - grated (2 cups)**
**1 boiled potato - mashed coarsely (½ cup)**
**½" piece fresh ginger - grated**
**salt to taste, ½ tsp red chilli powder**
**1 tsp roasted, ground cumin seeds (bhuna jeera)**
**¼ tsp amchoor**
**1 tbsp each of cashews (kaju) and raisins (kishmish) - chopped**
**2 green chillies - deseeded and finely chopped, ¼ tsp sugar**

1. Sift flour, semolina, salt and baking powder into a bowl. Rub in ghee or butter. Add a few tablespoons of cold water to form a firm dough.

Knead for 5-7 minutes until dough becomes smooth & elastic. Cover dough and keep aside for 30 minutes or longer while making the filling.

2. To prepare filling, heat 3 tbsp oil in a pan. Remove from heat. Add ginger, salt, red chilli powder, bhuna jeera and amchoor.

3. Return to heat. Add kaju and kishmish. Cook for a few seconds. Add potatoes. Stir for a few seconds. Add cauliflower. Mix well. Add sugar and green chillies.

4. Cover and cook on low heat till the cauliflower is cooked. Make the filling spicy if you like. Keep aside.

5. Make lemon sized balls of dough. Roll out into thin rounds. Cut each circle in half. Brush some water on straight edges. Pick up the half circle and form a cone shape, overlapping straight edges ¼" & pressing firmly to seal the seam. Fill cone two-thirds with filling, about 1 tbsp of the filling in each cone. Press together to make a secure joint.

6. Deep fry 8-10 pieces on low medium heat till golden. Drain on paper and serve with chutney.

**TIP:** Never fry samosas on high heat. Fry 8-10 pieces together in a single batch. If the oil is too hot, the outer covering gets browned very fast, without getting cooked properly.

# Purani Dilli Ke
# NASHTE AUR SNACKS

# Bervi Poori aur Aloo Chhole

*From the famous Kedarnath Premchand Halwai of Chandani Chowk. Serve the aloos with kachouri, samosa or crisp fried poories. An ultimate Sunday breakfast.*

*Makes 16-18*                    *Picture on cover*

**SUBZI**

**1½ cups kabuli channa (safeed choole) - soaked overnight for 6-8 hours**
**1 potato**
**¼ tsp cooking soda (soda-bi-carb)**
**4 tbsp oil/ghee**
**2 pinches of hing (asafoetida)**
**½ tsp jeera (cumin seeds), ½ tsp fenugreek seeds (methi daana)**
**1 green chilli - finely chopped**
**1 tsp ginger paste (1" piece of ginger - crushed to a paste)**
**½ tsp haldi, 1 tbsp dhania powder**
**1 tsp channa masala (readymade)**
**1½ tsp salt, ½ tsp amchoor, ½ tsp red chilli powder**
**1 tsp lemon juice, 2 tbsp coriander leaves - chopped**

## POORI (DOUGH)
**2 cups atta (whole wheat flour)**
**½ cup sooji (semolina) - soaked in 1 cup water, 2 tbsp ghee**

### FILLING OF POORI
**¾ cup dhuli urad ki dal (white dal), a pinch hing (asafoetida)**
**½ tsp saunf (fennel seeds), 2 tsp finely chopped ginger**
**3 tsp dhania powder, ¾ tsp red chilli powder, ½ tsp salt**

1. Soak the channa over night in some water. Drain water. Add 3 cups fresh water. Add soda. Mix well. Pressure cook till one whistle on high flame and then keep on low heat for 15 minutes. Remove from fire.
2. Boil & peel potato, then cut into 6 pieces. Keep aside.
3. For filling of puris, soak dal in 2 cups water for atleast 2-3 hours.
4. For the dough, soak sooji in 1 cup water for 1 hour.

5. For the subzi, heat 4 tsbp oil/ghee in a kadhai, reduce heat, add hing, jeera and methi daana. Do not let the methi seeds turn black. Add green chillies.
6. Then add the ginger paste and stir for 30 seconds. Add haldi, dhania powder and channa masala. Bhuno for 2 minutes.
7. Add potatoes and stir for 2-3 minutes. Add channas, salt, amchoor

and red chilli powder. Cook for 15 minutes on medium heat.

8. Add coriander and lemon juice. Remove from fire. Keep aside till serving time.

9. For the puris, mix atta with the soaked sooji. Add ghee and mix well. Knead into a dough as for poories. Keep the dough aside, covered with a moist napkin or cloth.

10. For the filling of poories, drain the soaked dal. Grind it to a paste in a mixer-grinder to a paste, using very little water if required.

11. Heat 2 tbsp ghee in a kadhai. Add hing and saunf. Wait till saunf starts to change colour. Add finely chopped ginger, dhania powder, red chilli powder and salt. Bhuno for 1 minute. Add the dal paste. Bhuno for 5 minutes. Let it cool.

12. Make small lemon sized balls of the dough. Roll out a little. Put 1 heaped teaspoon of dal filling. Make a ball again. Roll out to a puri.

13. Deep fry in hot oil. Serve with aloo-chole ki sabzi.

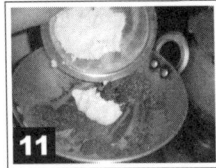

# Seviyaan Roll

*Makes 16*

**2½ cups boiled and grated aloo (4 potatoes)**
**2 slices bread - churned in a mixer to get fresh bread crumbs**
**½ cup chopped coriander, ½ tsp chaat masala**
**½ tsp bhuna jeera (roasted cumin powder)**
**1½ tsp salt, ½ tsp pepper, ½ tsp baking powder**
**2 tbsp melted butter**
**TO COAT**
**¼ cup maida, 1 cup very thin seviyaan- crushed roughly into small pieces by hand**

1. Mix grated potatoes, coriander, chaat masala, fresh bread crumbs, bhuna jeera, salt and pepper. Mix gently without applying too much pressure.

2. Sprinkle baking powder on the potatoes. Melt butter in a microwave or on fire and pour on the potatoes. Mix gently but very well.

3. Make 16 lemon sized balls. With a ball of mixture, make a long oval roll. Shape to give a neat roll.

4. Flatten the ends of the roll by making it stand upright on a flat platform. To neaten the roll, roll the aloo roll on the flat platform.

5. Break seviyaan into very small pieces. Spread on a plate. Spread maida also on a separate plate. Take 1 cup of water separately in a shallow flat bowl (katori).
6. Press the roll over maida to coat all over.
7. Dip the roll in the water for a second and then immediately roll it over the seviyaan. All the sides should be completely covered with seviyaan. Stick the seviyaan well.

8. Keep aside to set for atleast 15 minutes. Deep fry 2-3 pieces at a time. Serve with chutney.

# Chhole Bhature

*Awesome! I can never forget the channa bhaturas I used to have at 'Sadar Bazar' when I went for cracker shopping for my kids for Diwali.*

*Picture on facing page*                    *Serves 4*

## PRESSURE COOK TOGETHER
1 cup channa kabuli (Bengal gram), ¼ tsp soda- bi- carb (mitha soda)
2 moti illaichi (big cardamoms), 1" stick dalchini (cinnamon)
2 tsp tea leaves tied in a muslin cloth or 2 tea bags, 1 tsp salt

## MASALA
2 onions - chopped finely
1½ tsp anar daana (dry pomegranate seeds) - powdered
5 big tomatoes - chopped finely
1" piece ginger - chopped finely, 1 green chilli - chopped finely
1 tsp dhania powder, ½ tsp garam masala
½ tsp red chilli powder or to taste
2 tsp channa masala, 1¼ tsp salt or to taste

## BHATURE

**2 cups maida (plain flour), 1 cup suji (semolina)**
**½ tsp salt, ½ tsp sugar, ½ tsp soda-bicarb (mitha soda)**
**½ cup curd, (preferably a day old and slightly sour), oil for deep frying**

1. Soak channas overnight or for 6-8 hours in a pressure cooker. Next morning, discard water. Wash channas with fresh water and add mitha soda, moti illaichi, dalchini, tea leaves, 1 tsp salt and just enough water to cover the channas nicely.

2. Pressure cook all the ingredients together to give one whistle. After the first whistle, keep on low flame for about 15 minutes. Remove from fire. Keep aside.

3. Heat 4 tbsp oil. Add onions. Saute till transparent. Add anardaana powder. Cook stirring till onions turn brown. (Do not burn them).

4. Add chopped tomatoes, ginger and green chill. Stir fry for 5- 6 minutes.

5. Add dhania powder, garam masala and chilli powder. Mash and stir fry tomatoes occasionally for 8-10 minutes or till they turn brown in colour and oil separates.

6. Strain channas, reserving the liquid. Remove tea bag from the boiled channas.

*Contd...*

◁ *Kathi Roti : Recipe on page 41*

7. Add the strained channas to the onion-tomato masala. Mix well. Stir fry gently for 5-7 minutes.

8. Add channa masala. Add the channa liquid. Check salt and add a little to taste. Cook for 15-20 minutes on medium heat till the liquid dries up and still a saucy consistency remains. Keep aside.

9. For bhature, soak suji in ¾ cup warm water, which is just enough to cover it. Keep aside for 10 minutes.

10. Sift salt, sugar, soda and maida in a paraat or a shallow bowl.

11. Add sugar, soaked suji and curd. Mix very well. Add warm water little by little, mixing well till the dough collects in the centre. Knead well to make a firm dough. Do not make it loose as on keeping it turns loose.

12. Knead again with greased hands till the dough is smooth. Pat some oil on the dough to prevent it from drying. Grease a polythene with oil from inside and put the dough in it. Tie a knot loosely. Keep it in a warm place for 3-4 hours or till serving time.

13. Make 8-10 balls. Roll each ball to an oblong shape. Pull from one side to get a pointed tip. Deep fry in hot oil. Drain on paper napkins. Serve with channas.

# Kathi Roti

*These rolls are served with paneer-vegetable sticks. For a quicker version omit the paneer sticks and serve just the subzi with roomali roti, although the sticks definitely add to its taste. The sticks can be served separately as a snack too.*

*Serves 4*          *Picture on page 38*

**SUBZI**

1 cup nutri nugget granules - soaked for 1 hour and drained
½ cup matar (peas) - boiled
1 cup tomato puree, 1 tomato - chopped
1 onion - chopped
2 pinches of hing, ½ tsp jeera (cumin seeds)
1 dry saboot red chilli - crushed
½ tsp garm masala, 1 tbsp dhania powder, 1 tsp salt
½ tsp amchoor, ¼ tsp red chilli powder
1 green chilli - finely chopped, juice of ½ lemon
1 tsp ginger-garlic paste, 2 tbsp pao bhaji masala
2 tbsp coriander leaves - chopped

*Contd...*

**PANEER-VEG STICKS**

**125 gms paneer- cut into ½" thick slices and then into ¾" squares**
**1 capsicum- cut into 1" pieces**
**1 tomato - cut into 4 pieces lengthwise, pulp removed and cut into 1"**
**pieces some chaat masala**
**BATTER**
**1 cup besan (gramflour), 1/3 cup water - approx**
**2 pinches baking powder**
**¾ tsp each red chilli powder and salt,or to taste**
**1 green chilli - chopped very finely**

1. For the subzi, soak the nuti nuggets in 1 cup water, keep aside for ½ hour. Strain through a soup strainer. Wash several times with water in the strainer itself. Press the nuggets in the strainer, squeezing out excess water from the nuggets.
2. Heat 4 tbsp ghee or oil in a kadhai, add hing, jeera, green chillies and saboot sookhi lal mirch. Wait for 30 seconds.
3. Add chopped onion and cook till golden.
4. Add the nutri nuggets granules and bhuno for 5 minutes.
5. Add the peas, ginger paste, dhania powder, salt, pao bhaji masala

and chopped tomatoes. Bhuno for 5 minutes.

6. Add tomato puree, red chilli powder and amchoor. Mix well and cook for 5 minutes.

7. Add 1 cup water mix thoroughly. Give one boil. Simmer for 5 minutes till a semi dry masala is ready. Add coriander and mix. Remove from fire.

8. For sticks, make a thick batter with all ingredients. Beat well and keep aside for 10 minutes.

9. Sprinkle chat masala nicely on paneer, capsicum & tomato pieces. Mix lightly.

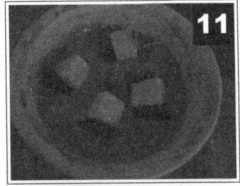

10. Thread a capsicum (wrong side facing you), then a paneer and then a tomato piece (right side facing you) on each tooth pick. Keep aside till serving time.

11. Heat oil for deep frying. Dip the paneer sticks in the prepared batter. Coat well with the fingers, sticking the batter nicely. Deep fry till golden.

12. To serve, sprinkle sticks with some chaat masala. Add lemon juice to the subzi. Serve subzi topped with a hot stick with roomali roti.

# Mattar Kachouri aur Subzi

*Enjoy this subzi with kachouris, poories or paranthas! It's good fun to have it with buttered toasts for breakfast too.*

*Picture on inside front cover*　　Makes 12-14

### DOUGH FOR KACHOURI
**2 cups maida (flour)**
**½ tsp baking powder, ½ tsp salt, 2 tbsp ghee**
**½ cup warm water to knead, approx.**

### FILLING
**2 cups peas (matar) - shelled**
**1 tbsp ghee**
**2 pinches of hing (asafoetida)**
**¼ tsp jeera (cumin seeds), 1 tsp dhania powder**
**¼ tsp haldi (turmeric powder)**
**¼ tsp grated ginger**
**1 green chilli - deseeded and chopped**
**1 tsp salt, ¼ tsp red chilli powder, ¾ tsp chaat masala**

¾ tsp amchoor, ¾ tsp garam masala
2 tbsp besan (gramflour)

**SUBZI**
**6 potatoes - boiled, peeled and cut into 5-6 pieces, mash the pieces**
**roughly**
**3½ tbsp ghee or oil**
**3 pinches of hing (asafoetida)**
**¾ tsp jeera (cumin seeds), 1 tsp saunf (fennel)**
**¼ tsp methi dana (fenugreek seeds)**
**½ tsp haldi powder, 1 tsp dhania powder**
**1½ tsp salt, ¾ tsp red chilli powder**
**1 tbsp aam ke achar ka masala**
**1 green chilli - finely chopped**
**2 tbsp chopped coriander (hara dhania)**
**1 tsp very finely chopped or grated ginger**

1. To prepare the dough, sift maida, baking powder and salt through a sieve (channi).

*Contd...*

2. Add ghee and mix well till it appears like bread crumbs. Knead well with warm water into a soft dough. Keep aside for 20 minutes.
3. For the filling, boil 4-5 cups water with 1 tsp salt and 1 tsp sugar. Add peas to boiling water. As soon as the boil returns, remove from fire. Let peas be in hot water for 15 minutes. Strain and keep aside. Mash lightly with the back of a big spoon or a potato masher.
4. Heat ghee in a kadhai, add hing and jeera. Reduce heat. When jeera turns golden, add dhania powder, haldi and grated ginger. Bhuno for 1 minute.
5. Add the chopped green chillies, mix and cook for 2 minutes.
6. Add peas to the above masala in the kadhai, mix well and bhuno till golden, for about 10 minutes on low heat.
7. Add the salt, red chilli powder, chaat masala, amchoor, garam masala and besan.
   Bhuno for another 2 minutes. Remove from fire. Cool the filling.
8. With the dough, make small puries and fill each with 1 tbsp mattar masala. Cover to form a ball and flatten it slightly.
9. Heat oil in a kadhai and deep fry 5-6 pieces at a time. The oil should

be hot when you first drop the kachouries in oil, then lower flame and cook till they turn brown.

10. For the subzi, heat ghee in a kadhai. Reduce heat and add hing, jeera, saunf and methi dana.

11. When methi dana turns brown, add haldi, dhania powder and salt. Bhuno for 1 minute on low heat.

12. Add achar ka masala. Stir for another 1 minute.

13. Add the potatoes, chopped green chilli, coriander and ginger. Stir fry on medium heat for 3-4 minutes.

14. Add 3 cups of water. Bring to a boil. Reduce heat and cook for another 10 minutes. Remove from fire. Serve hot.

**Variation : Aloo Hing Kachouri**

Use 2 medium sized potatoes - boiled and grated instead of matar, for the filling. Rest all the ingredients remain the same. Proceed in the same way as for matar kachouri.

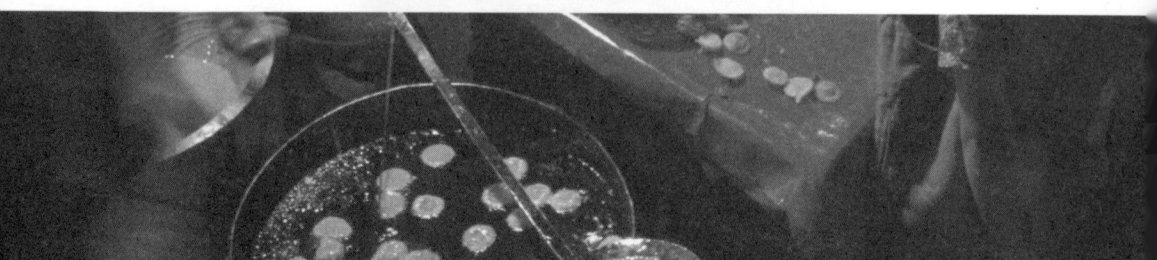

# Dilli Walon Ki SUBZIYAN

# Karari Arvi

*Serves 6*

**½ kg arvi (colocassia)**
**1½ tsp ajwain (carom seeds), 2-3 pinches of hing (asafoetida)**
**1½ tsp salt, ¾ tsp red chilli powder, oil for frying**

1. Put the arvi in a presure cooker. Add enough water to cover the arbi. Pressure cook to give 1 whistle. Reduce heat and cook for 2 minutes on low heat. Remove from fire and let the pressure drop by itself.
2. Peel the arvi and cut each into 2 pieces lengthwise. Flatten each piece.
3. Heat oil for frying in a kadhai. Deep fry arvi in 3-4 batches till golden brown. Remove from oil.
4. Heat 3 tbsp oil. Add ajwain and shut off the flame. Ad hing, salt and red chilli powder. Return to fire. Stir.
5. Add fried arvi. Mix very well. Reduce heat. Cover and cook on low heat for 5 minutes, stirring once or twice in between. Serve.

# Dal ki Pakori

*Picture on page 1*                    *Serves 5-6*

**½ cup (200 gm) dhuli mung ki dal (husked green beans)**
**½ cup channe ki dal, ½ tsp salt, ½ tsp eno fruit salt**

**GRAVY**
**1 onion - chopped, 1 onion and 1" piece of giner and 6- 8 flakes of garlic-**
**ground to a paste in a mixer, 1 tsp salt, ½ tsp garam masala**
**1½ tsp dhania powder, ½ tsp haldi powder, ½ tsp red chilli powder**
**¼ tsp amchoor, 2 tomatoes - blanched (put in boiling water for 2-3**
**minutes and peeled) and pureed, 2 tbsp chopped coriander**

1. Wash dals and soak in water overnight.
2. Next day drain dals and grind them to a rough paste in a mixer grinder. Do not make it into a smooth paste. Beat ground dal in a bowl with an electric hand mixer for 5-7 minutes till it feels really light and frothy. To check it it is done put a small ball in a bowl of water. If it rises to the surface, it is done, otherwise beat some more. Add eno fruit salt and salt. Mix well.

3. Heat oil in a kadhai for deep frying. To test if oil is hot enough, drop a little paste into the kadhai. It should rise to the surface almost immediately.

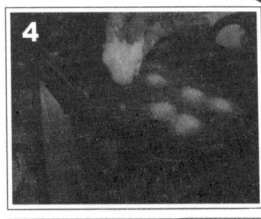

4. Using wet fingers drop small amounts of paste into oil. Reduce heat to medium. When bubbles appear on the surface and they swell a little, turn and fry till golden yellow. Drain and keep aside.

5. For gravy, heat 4 tbsp oil or ghee. Add chopped onion, fry till golden.
6. Add onion paste. Stir for 3-4 minutes on low heat.
7. Add all masalas. Stir on low heat for 1-2 minutes.
8. Add tomato puree. Stir on low heat for 7-8 minutes.
9. Add 4 cups water. Bring to a boil. Cook curry on low heat for 5 minutes.
10. At serving time, add the fried pakories and fresh coriander. Boil. Cover and cook for 4-5 minutes on low heat. The gravy should be quite thin.

# Shahi Paneer

*Serves 4*

**250 gm paneer - cut into 1" cubes, 5 large (500 gm) tomatoes**
**2 tbsp desi ghee or butter and 2 tbsp oil**
**4-5 flakes garlic and 1" piece ginger - ground to a paste**
**1 tbsp kasoori methi (dry fenugreek leaves), 1 tsp tomato ketchup**
**½ tsp jeera (cumin seeds), 2 tsp dhania powder, ½ tsp garam masala**
**1 tsp salt, or to taste, ½ tsp red chilli powder, preferably degi mirch**
**½ cup water, ½-1 cup milk, approx., ½ cup cream (optional)**
**3 tbsp cashewnuts (kaju)**

1. Soak kaju in a little warm water for 10-15 minutes.
2. Drain kaju. Grind in a mixer to a smooth paste with 2 tbsp water.
3. Cut each tomato into 4 pieces. Boil tomatoes in ½ cup water. Simmer for 4-5 minutes on low heat till tomatoes turn soft. Remove from fire and cool. Cut each into 4 pieces. Grind the tomatoes along with the water to a smooth puree.
4. Heat oil and ghee or butter in a kadhai. Reduce heat. Add jeera. When it turns golden, add ginger-garlic paste.

5. When paste starts to change colour add the above tomato puree and cook till dry.

6. Add kasoori methi and tomato ketchup.
7. Add dhania powder, garam masala, salt and red chilli powder. Mix well. Cook for 2 minutes or till oil seperates.
8. Add cashew paste. Mix well for 2 minutes.
9. Add water. Boil. Simmer on low heat for 4-5 minutes. Reduce heat.

10. Add the paneer cubes. Remove from fire. Keep aside to cool for about 5 minutes.
11. Add enough milk to the cold paneer masala to get a thick curry, mix gently. (Remember to add milk only after the masala is no longer hot, to prevent the milk from curdling. After adding milk, heat curry on low heat.)
12. Heat on low heat. Stir continuously till just about to boil.
13. Add cream, keeping the heat very low and stirring continuously. Remove from fire immediately and transfer to a serving dish. Swirl 1 tbsp cream over the hot paneer in the dish. Serve immediately.

# Anghiti Tamatar

*Picture on facing page*     *Serves 4*

4-5 medium sized tomatoes - washed
½ onion - finely chopped, 1 tbsp butter
¼ cup peas (matar), ½ cup finely chopped carrot
¾ tsp dhania powder, ½ tsp garam masala, ¼ red chilli powder
¼ tsp haldi powder, ½ tsp salt, ½ cup grated paneer
**GRAVY**
2 onions - sliced, 1 tomato - chopped
1" piece ginger - chopped (1 tbsp)
1 tsp salt, 1 tsp dhania powder, ½ tsp garam masala
¼ tsp amchoor, ¼ tsp red chilli powder, or to taste

1. From the stem side of the tomato, cut a piece like a lid and scoop out the pulp. Keep the lid aside. Rub the inside with a little salt, turn tomato upside down and leave for 10 minutes.

2. Heat 1 tbsp butter in a kadhai. Add chopped onion and bhuno till golden. Add the peas and carrots, dhania powder, garam masala, red

chilli powder, haldi powder and salt. Cover and cook on medium flame for 5-7 minutes or till peas are cooked. Add the grated paneer. Remove from heat.

3. Fill this mixture in the tomatoes. Put the lid back. Secure with a toothpick. Hold each tomato on the flame with the help of tongs and roast for 3- 4 minutes till black patches appear. Repeat with the remaining tomatoes.

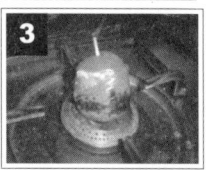

4. For the gravy, heat 4 tbsp oil and add sliced onions. Stir till golden brown. Add chopped tomatoes and ginger and cook for 7 minutes till tomatoes turn soft.

5. Add all masalas and cook for 2 minutes. Remove from fire and cool. Blend to a paste in a mixer grinder with ½ cup water.

6. Put prepared onion - tomato paste back in the same kadhai and stir for 4- 5 minutes on low heat. Add enough warm water (1 cup) to get a thin gravy. Boil. Simmer for 5-7 minutes till you get a thick gravy and oil separates. Keep aside.

7. To serve, boil gravy and add the tomatoes. Give 1-2 quick boils. Serve.

◁ *Gobhi Fry : Recipe on page 58*

# Gobhi Fry

*Picture on page 56*                    *Serves 4*

**1 medium whole cauliflowers (500 gms) - cut into medium size florets with stalks**

**MASALA**
**3 onions - chopped**
**3 tomatoes - roughly chopped**
**1" ginger - chopped**
**seeds of 1 moti illaichi**
**3-4 saboot kali mirch (peppercorns)**
**2 laung (cloves)**
**2 tbsp curd - beat well till smooth**
**½ tsp red chilli powder, ½ tsp garam masala**
**½ tsp haldi, ½ tsp amchoor**
**1 tsp salt, or to taste**

1. Break the cauliflower into medium size florets, keeping the stalk intact. Wash and pat dry on a kitchen towel.
2. Heat oil in a kadhai for deep frying. Add all the cauliflower pieces and

fry to a light brown colour. Remove from oil and keep aside.

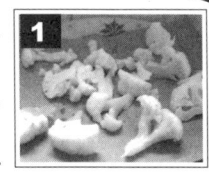

3. Heat 4 tbsp oil in a clean kadhai. Add chopped onion. Cook till onions turn golden brown.

4. Add moti illaichi, saboot kali mirch and laung. After a minute add chopped tomatoes and ginger. Cook for 4-5 minutes till they turn soft and masala turns little dry.

5. Add well beaten curd. Cook till masala turns reddish again.

6. Reduce heat. Add red chilli powder, garam masala, haldi, amchoor and salt. Cook for 1 minute. Add ½ cup water to get a thick masala. Boil. Cook for 1 minute on low flame. Keep aside.

7. At the time of serving, heat the masala. Add the fried cauliflower pieces to the masala and mix well on low heat for 2 minutes till the vegetable gets well blended with the masala. Serve hot.

# Dum Aloo

*Serves 4-6*

**POTATOES**
20 small baby potatoes or 4 medium round potatoes - cut into 1" pieces

**GRAVY**
1 tej patta, 1 tsp shah jeera (black cumin)
4 tbsp very finely grated khoya
1½ tbsp kasoori methi (dry fenugreek leaves)
1½ tsp salt or to taste, ½ tsp garam masala

**ONION PASTE (GRIND TOGETHER)**
1 onion, 2 laung, ¾" piece of ginger, 4-5 flakes of garlic
seeds of 2 chhoti illaichi, 2 tsp saunf
seeds of 2 moti illaichi, 1" stick dalchini

**TOMATO PASTE (GRIND TOGETHER)**
4 tomatoes - blanched (boiled in hot water for 3-4 minutes and peeled)
¼ tsp jaiphal, ¼ tsp javitri, 2 dry, red chillies, 2 tbsp kaju (cashewnuts)

1. Peel and wash the potatoes. Prick with a fork. Cut into 1" pieces, if using regular potatoes.

2. Keep the potatoes in salted water for 15 minutes. Strain and pat dry on a clean kitchen towel.
3. Heat oil. Deep fry all potatoes together till they get cooked properly & are golden brown in colour. Take out 1 piece from oil & check to see if cooked. If done, then remove all pieces from the kadhai on paper napkins. Keep aside till serving time.
4. Grind all the ingredients of onion paste to a smooth paste. Keep aside.
5. Boil tomatoes in water for 3-4 minutes. Peel. Grind all the ingredients of tomato paste to a smooth paste. Keep aside.
6. Heat 3 tbsp oil, add tej patta and shah jeera, wait for a minute.
7. Add onion paste. Cook for 2-3 minutes till golden brown.
8. Add tomato paste. Stir for 8-10 min or till dry.
9. Add khoya, kasoori methi, salt and garam masala. Cook for 2 minutes, stirring. Add ¾ cup of water. Boil. Simmer for 3 minutes. Remove from fire and keep aside till serving time.
10. At serving time, add 1 cup milk and boil on low heat.
11. Add fried potatoes. Keep on fire for 2-3 minutes. Serve hot.

# Dal Makhani

*Serves 4-5*

**1 cup urad saboot (whole black beans), 2 tbsp desi ghee**
**1½ tsp salt, 5 cups of water, 1 cup ready made tomato puree**
**¼ tsp jaiphal powder, ½ tsp garam masala**
**1½ tbsp kasoori methi (dry fenugreek leaves)**
**2-3 tbsp butter, preferably white**

**GRIND TO A PASTE**
**2 dry, whole red chillies, preferably Kashmiri red chillies - deseeded &**
**soaked for 10 minutes and then drained**
**1" piece ginger, 6-8 flakes garlic**

**ADD LATER**
**½ cup milk mixed with ½ cup cream or well beaten malai**

1. Wash the dal, and soak in warm water for atleast 2-3 hours.
2. Drain water. Wash several times in fresh water, rubbing well, till the water no longer remains black.

3. Pressure cook dal with 5 cups water, 2 tbsp ghee, salt and ginger-garlic-chilli paste. After the first whistle, keep on low flame for 30 minutes. Remove from fire.

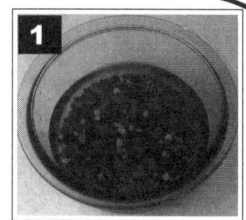

4. After the pressure drops, mash the hot dal a little. Keep aside.

5. To the dal in the cooker, add tomato puree, kasoori methi, garam masala and jaiphal powder.

6. Add butter. Simmer on medium flame for 30 minutes, stirring dal occasionally. Remove from fire. Keep aside to cool till the time of serving.

7. At the time of serving, add milk mixed with cream to the dal. Keep dal on fire and bring to a boil on low heat, stirring constantly. Mix very well with a karchhi. Simmer for 2 minutes more, to get the right colour and smoothness. Remove from fire. Serve.

**Note:** Originally the dal was cooked by leaving it overnight on the burning coal angithis. The longer the dal simmered, the better it tasted.

# Sabut Simla Mirch

*Picture on facing page*          *Serves 4*

4 small capsicums
1 onion - finely chopped
3 potatoes - boiled and mashed roughly
2 tsp grated ginger
1 green chilli - finely chopped, 2 tbsp chopped coriander
3 tbsp oil
1 tsp jeera (cumin seeds)
½ tsp haldi, 1 tsp dhania powder, ¼ tsp amchoor, ½ tsp garam masala
½ tsp red chilli powder, ¾ tsp salt, or taste
a few tooth picks

1. Wash and cut a slice from the top of each capsicum like a small lid. Keep the lids with their respective capsicums. (Do not mix all the lids).
2. Heat 3 tbsp oil in a kadhai. Add jeera. When it turns golden, add onions. Stir fry till golden. Add ginger, stir fry for 1 minute.

3. Add haldi, dhania, amchoor, garam masala, red chilli powder and salt.

4. Add mashed potatoes, green chilli and coriander. Mix well and bhuno for another 4-5 minutes. Remove from fire and cool.
5. Stuff this mixture in the capsicum. Place lids back. Secure lids with tooth picks.
6. In a kadhai/pan put 2 tbsp oil and shallow fry the capsicums on low heat for about 15 minutes. Keep them spread out, turning sides occassionally, till the skin becomes brownish at some places and changes colour and becomes soft. Serve hot.

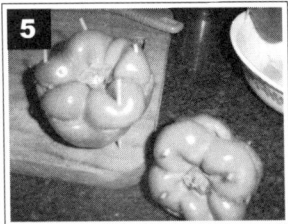

◁ *Sarson ka Saag : Recipe on page 72*
◁ *Makki ki Roti : Recipe on page 79*

# Dilli Style Sukhe Aloo

*Serves 3 -4*

**4 large potatoes - boiled, peeled and each cut into 8-12 pieces (1" cubes)**
**¾ tsp garam masala**
**½ tsp amchoor powder**
**2 tsp dhania powder**
**½ tsp haldi powder**
**½ tsp bhuna jeera powder (roasted cumin powder)**
**1¼ tsp salt or to taste**

**OTHER INGREDIENTS**
**4 tbsp oil**
**1 tsp jeera (cumin seeds)**
**1 tsp finely chopped ginger, 1 tsp finely chopped garlic**
**2 onions - thinly sliced**
**2 green chillies - cut into thin long pieces**
**3-4 tbsp coriander leaves - finely chopped, 1 tsp lemon juice**

1. Cut potatoes into medium sized cubes.
2. Heat 4 tbsp oil in kadhai, reduce heat and add jeera. When it starts to change colour, add ginger and garlic. Stir for ½ minute.
3. Add sliced onion and fry till onions turn golden brown.
4. Add green chilli pieces, stir for 1 minute.
5. Add the potatoes, garam masala, amchoor powder, dhania powder, haldi powder, bhuna jeera powder and salt.
6. Stir for 8- 10 minutes, stirring only occasionally. Too frequent stirring does not let the potatoes turn crisp. Keep the potatoes spread out while cooking. Check salt. Remove from fire.
7. Serve sprinkled with lemon juice and chopped coriander leaves.

# Bharwan Karela

*Serves 4-6*

**(300 gms) 6 karela (bitter gourd)**
**2 tsp salt, 3 tbsp vinegar oil for deep frying, thread for tying the karelas**
**MASALA**
**1 tbsp saunf (fennel seeds) - powdered**
**1½ onions - finely chopped, ½ of the scrapings (peel of the karelas)**
**½ tsp haldi, ½ tsp garam masala, 2 tsp amchoor, 2 tsp dhania powder**
**½ tsp salt, ¼ tsp red chilli powder, ¼ tsp sugar**
**1 tbsp achaar ka masala, preferably aam ke achaar ka masala**

1. Scrape the karele. Preserve the scrappings (peel) for the filling. Mix half of the scrappings with 1 tsp salt. Keep aside. Throw away the rest of the peels (scrappings).
2. Slit the karela and remove the seeds.
3. Rub salt within and outside the karela liberally. Sprinkle 2 tbsp vinegar on the karelas and rub the karelas well.
4. Boil 5-6 cups water with 2 tsp salt. Put karelas in water and boil for 2

minutes. Remove from fire. Strain. Pick up the karelas and squeeze to remove bitterness. Wash again, squeeze and keep karelas aside. Wash scrapings well, squeezing well to remove the bitterness. Wash several times and squeeze well.

5. For masala, heat 3 tbsp oil in the kadhai, add onion, fry a little till it starts to turn golden. Add the washed and squeezed scrapping. Stir for 4-5 minutes till dry.

6. Add haldi, garam masala, amchoor, dhania powder, salt, red chilli powder sugar and aam ke achaar ka masala. Bhuno for another 5 minutes on low flame, stirring continuously.

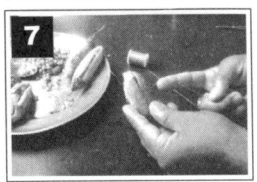

7. Stuff the above mixture in the karelas and tie it with a thread to seal the filling.

8. Heat 1 cup oil for frying. Add the tied karelas and shallow fry for 5-7 minutes, turning sides till reddish brown on medium heat. Serve hot with paranthas and dal fry.

# Sarson Ka Saag

*Picture on page 66*          *Serves 6*

**1 bundle (1 kg) sarson (green mustard)**
**250 gm spinach (palak) or baathoo**
**2 shalgam (turnips) - peeled and chopped, optional**
**3-4 flakes garlic - finely chopped, optional**
**2" piece ginger - finely chopped**
**1 green chilli - chopped, ¾ tsp salt, or to taste**
**2 tbsp makki ka atta (maize flour)**
**1½ tsp powdered gur (jaggery)**

**TADKA/TEMPERING**
**3 tbsp desi ghee, 2 green chillies - finely chopped**
**1" piece ginger - finely chopped, ½ tsp red chilli powder**

1. Wash and clean mustard leaves. First remove the leaves and then peel the stems, starting from the lower end and chop them finely. (Peel stems the way you string green beans). The addition of stems to the saag

makes it tastier but it is important to peel the stems from the lower ends. The upper tender portion may just be chopped. Chop the spinach or baathoo leaves and mix with sarson.

2. Put chopped greens with ½ cup water in a pan.
3. Chop garlic, ginger and green chilli very finely and add to the saag, add shalgam if you wish. Add salt and put it on fire and let it start heating.
4. The saag will start going down. Cover and let it cook on medium fire for 15-20 minutes. Remove from fire, cool.
5. Grind to a rough paste. Do not grind too much.
6. Add makki ka atta to the saag and cook for 15 minutes on low heat.
7. At serving time, heat desi ghee. Reduce heat and add ginger & green chillies. Cook till ginger changes colour. Remove from fire and add red chilli powder. Add ghee to the hot saag and mix lightly. Serve hot.
8. Serve with fresh home made butter and makki- ki-roti.

**Note:** When buying sarson, see that the saag has tender leaves and tender stems (gandal).

# Baingan ka Bharta

*Picture on facing page*          *Serves 3-4*

**1 medium baingan (brinjal) of round variety (350 gm)**
**2 onions - chopped finely**
**½ cup ready-made tomato puree, 1 tomato - chopped**
**½" piece ginger - chopped finely, 1 green chilli - chopped**
**2 tsp dhania (coriander) powder, ¼ tsp haldi, ½ tsp garam masala**
**½ tsp degi mirch or red chilli powder, 1 tsp salt**

1. Rub 1 tbsp oil all over the baingan and roast over a gas flame until the skin gets charred and starts to peel off and flesh is soft.
2. Remove the charred skin from the brinjal. Mash the flesh with a fork and keep pulp aside.
3. In a kadhai, heat 3- 4 tbsp oil add onions, ginger and green chilli. Cook till onions turn golden brown.
4. Add dhania, haldi, garam masala & degi mirch. Cook for 5 minutes.
5. Add mashed brinjal and bhuno for 10 minutes.
6. Add chopped tomato and tomato puree and 1 tsp salt. Mix well. Cook for 5- 6 minutes. Serve hot.

# Dal Fry

*Serves 4*

**¼ cup arhar dal, ¾ cup channa dal, 3½ cups water**
**½ tsp haldi, 1½ tsp salt, 1 tsp kasoori methi, 1 tsp ghee**
**TADKA**
**3-4 tbsp ghee, ½ tsp tsp jeera, a pinch of hing, 2 tomatoes - chopped**
**1 onion - finely chopped, 1 tsp finely chopped ginger**
**½ tsp garam masala, 1 tsp dhania powder, 1/8 tsp amchoor**
**½ tsp red chilli powder, preferably degi mirch**
**1 tsp kasoori methi (dry fenugreek leaves), 1-2 whole green chillies**

1. Clean and wash dals together in 2-3 changes of water. Add water, salt, haldi, kasoori methi. Pressure cook to give 1 whistle. Keep on low heat for 5 minutes. Remove from fire. Let pressure drop by itself.
2. For tadka, heat ghee in a kadhai. Reduce heat. Add jeera. when it starts changing colour, add hing, garlic. Wait for for 30 seconds.
3. Add tomatoes. Stir for 2 minutes. Add masalas and kasoori methi. Mix well for 3-4 minutes on low heat. Add green chillies. Mix well.
5. Pour over the hot dal and mix. Serve hot.

◁ *Gobhi Samosa : Recipe on page 28*

# Sukhi Urad Dal

*Serves 4*

**1 cup dhuli urad (split black beans) - soaked for 20 minutes**
**1 tbsp oil, ½ tsp jeera (cumin seeds), ½ tsp haldi, 1¼ tsp salt**
**¼ tsp garam masala, ¼ tsp dhania powder, ¼ tsp red chilli powder**
**TEMPRING/TADKA**
**3 tbsp desi ghee/oil, a pinch of hing, ½ tsp jeera (cumin seeds)**
**1 onion - sliced very finely, ¼ tsp red chilli powder**
**1-2 whole, dry, red chillies - broken into 2 pieces**

1. Strain the soaked dal and keep aside.
2. Heat 1 tbsp oil in a cooker. Reduce heat, add jeera. Let it turn golden.
3. Add dal. Stir to mix. Add haldi, salt, garam masala, dhania powder and red chilli powder. Stir on low flame for 1 minute.
4. Add 1 cup water. Pressure cook to give 1 whistle. Keep on low flame for 1 minute only. Remove from fire. Let the pressure drop by itself.
5. For tadka, heat oil in a pan. Add hing & jeera. Add onions & cook till brown. Add chilli powder and whole red chillies. Immediately remove from fire and pour the tadka over the hot dal. Mix gently. Serve hot.

# ROTIYAAN AUR CHAAWAL

## Makki ki Roti

*Serves 4*

*Picture on page 66*

**2 cups makai ka atta (maize flour)**
**hot water - to knead, ghee or oil for frying**

1. Sieve the flour. Knead gently with hot water to a soft dough. Do not knead the dough too much in advance.
2. Tear an old polythene bag into two halves. Keep one piece on the chakla (rolling board). Put one ball of the kneaded dough on the polythene. Cover with the other piece, such that there is a plastic cover above and beneath the ball.
3. Now roll carefully with a rolling pin (belan) to a slightly thick roti.
4. Cook the roti on both sides on a griddle. Put some ghee and fry on low flame.

# Varqi Parantha

*Makes 8*

**2½ cups (250 gm) flour (maida), 1½ tsp salt**
**3-4 tbsp thick malai or thick cream, ½ tsp sugar, 2 drops of kewra essence**
**1 tbsp melted ghee**

**LAYERING**
**3 tbsp ghee, 3 tbsp maida**

1. Sieve flour and salt in a mixing bowl or a parat.
2. Mix cream and sugar in a small bowl. Add kewra essence and stir.
3. Add the malai mixture to the maida and mix well. Knead with just enough water, adding about ¾ cup water gradually to make a firm smooth dough. Smear the prepared dough with some ghee to prevent it from drying, and cover well with a cloth napkin. Keep aside for 30-45 minutes.
4. Add 1 tbsp melted ghee to the dough. Mix well. Knead till smooth. Cover and again keep aside for 15 minutes.
5. Place dough on a lightly floured big surface like a kitchen platform.

Roll out the dough into a big rectangular shape (like a tray) of about 12" long and 10" broad. Apply 1 tbsp ghee evenly over the rolled out dough, sprinkle 1 tbsp flour all over.

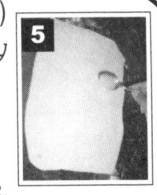

6. Fold about 4" (about 1/3) from top.
7. Fold the bottom over to get a strip with 3 folds.
8. Wrap strip of dough in a cloth napkin and keep in a plate. Put in the freezer of the refrigerator for 15 minutes. Take it out, roll it out again and fold in the same way as above and keep in the freezer wrapped in a cloth for another 15 minutes.

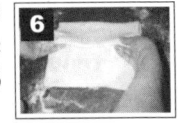

9. Remove from refrigerator, place on the floured surface, roll out again like a tray.

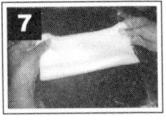

10. Cut small discs of 4" diameter with a round cutter or lid of any container.
11. Heat a tawa. Roll out cut discs (parantha) to the thickness you like. Put on hot tawa and cook both sides lightly. Pour some ghee on the sides and on top. Fry pressing sides with a paper tissue, till golden and cooked. Serve hot.

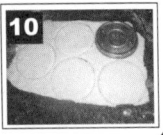

# Mashoor Bharwaan Paranthe

*In the famous 'Paranthe Waali Gali' in Chandani Chowk, I saw the paranthas being stuffed with the masala or gobhi filling and then the filling being sprinkled with some dry flour. I wondered why the flour was being sprinkled on the filling and the next moment I guessed the reason. The flour absorbs any moisture present in the filling and thus makes the paranthas really crisp! Keep the paranthas a little thick with lots of filling inside.*

### Makes 8

**FILLING**
2½ cups grated cauliflower (1 big flower) or paneer
2 tbsp coriander - very finely chopped
1 tsp grated ginger, 1 tsp amchoor, 1 tsp garam masala
1 tsp red chilli powder, 2 tsp salt

**DOUGH**
2 cups atta (whole wheat flour), ½ tsp salt
about ¾ cups water to knead

1. Prepare the dough by adding enough water to atta and salt. Cover and keep aside for 30 minutes.
2. Mix all ingredients of the filling lightly.
3. Take a big lemon sized ball of the dough. Roll it out to the size of a roti.

4. On the roti, put 3 tbsp of cauliflower, leaving 1" from all around. Sprinkle 1 tbsp of dry atta on it. Fold from all sides and make a ball again with the stuffing. Flatten ball and press on some dry flour to coat both sides.
5. Roll out to a round parantha. Keep the parantha thick, do not roll out too much.
6. Sprinkle a pinch of salt and red chilli powder on the parantha. Press with a belan (rolling pin).
7. Heat 2-3 tbsp ghee on a tawa. Shallow fry the parantha in ghee on the tawa till crisp on both sides. Trickle ghee from the sides while frying. Serve hot.

# Katluma Parantha

*A layered parantha.*

*Makes 10*

**3 cups maida (plain flour)**
**6 tbsp ghee plus ghee for frying**
**½ tsp salt**
**½ tsp red chilli powder**
**2 tbsp maida (plain flour)**

1. Sift maida with salt. Gradually add enough water (about ¾ cup) to make a dough of rolling consistency. Cover dough with a cloth napkin. Keep aside for 30 min.
2. Melt 2 tbsp ghee and knead into the dough. Knead very well till the dough is soft and elastic.
3. To the remaining ghee mix 2 tbsp flour and make a paste of ghee and maida.

4. Make 10 balls. Roll out each to make a thick chappati.
5. Spread some ghee-maida paste all over.
6. Fold into half, again spread the ghee paste. Again fold into half to get a long strip.

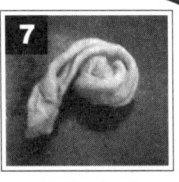

7. Roll the strip like a pinwheel, to get a pedha (round flattened ball).
8. Keep the peda upright on the palm. Flatten it between the palms of the hands or gently roll on the chakla (rolling board) with the belan (rolling pin) without applying too much pressure, to a small thick parantha of about 6" diameter.

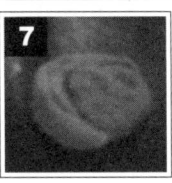

9. Put some ghee on the tawa. Heat ghee and put the parantha on the tawa. Trickle some ghee from the sides. Fry till rich brown on both sides on medium low heat. Press the sides and all over the parantha with a spoon while frying to ensure that it gets cooked since the parantha is a little thick.
10. Remove from tawa on to a clean kitchen napkin and press the hot parantha on the cloth from all sides for the layers to open up and turn flaky. Serve hot.

# Nan Badaami

## Makes 6

**2½ cups (250 gm) maida (plain flour)**
**½ cup hot milk, 1 tsp baking powder, ½ cup warm water (approx.)**
**½ tsp salt, 10 badaam (almonds) - cut into long thin pieces (slivered)**

1. Heat milk and put it in a big bowl. Add baking powder to the hot milk. Mix well & keep it aside for 1-2 minutes.
2. Sift maida and salt together. Add maida to the hot milk. Mix.
3. Knead to a dough with enough warm water. Keep in a warm place for 3-4 hours.
4. Make 6-8 balls. Roll out each ball to an oblong shape. Spread ghee all over.
5. Sprinkle some chopped almonds. Press with a rolling pin (belan). Pull one side of the nan to give it a pointed end like the shape of the nan.
6. Apply some water on the back side of the nan. Stick in a hot tandoor.
7. Cook till nan is ready. Spread butter on the ready nan and serve hot.

# Paneer Waala Bhatura

*Serves 4*

**2 cups (250 gms) maida (plain flour), 1 cup (100 gms) suji (semolina)**
**½ tsp soda-bicarb (mitha soda), ½ tsp salt, 1 tsp sugar**
**½ cup curd, preferably 1 day old, oil for deep frying**
**FILLING**
**75 gms paneer - mashed**
**½ tsp salt, ¾ tsp red chilli powder, ½ tsp garam masala**

1. Soak suji in water, which is just enough to cover it.
2. Sift salt, soda and maida. Add sugar, curd and the soaked suji. Knead with enough warm water to make a dough of rolling consistency.
3. Knead again with greased hands till the dough is smooth.
4. Brush the dough with oil.
5. Keep dough in greased polythene. Keep it in a warm place for 4 hours.
6. Make 8-10 balls. Roll out, put 1 tbsp of filling. Cover the filling with the dough to form a ball again.
7. Roll each ball to an oblong shape, and deep fry in hot oil till crisp and light golden.

# Ab Kuch Khaas
## MEETHA

## Daryaganj ka Rabri Falooda

*Serves 4*

**2 cups falooda or rice seviyan - broken into short lengths, 1" pieces**
**4 cups rabri - chilled, recipe given on next page**
**2 cups crushed ice, ½ cup rose syrup**

1. Boil the falooda or seviyan in water for about 2-3 minutes until soft. Drain and refresh in cold water. Keep covered in the refrigerator till serving time.
2. To serve, take a tall glass. Put ½ cup rabri. Top with ½ cup crushed ice. Pour 2 tbsp of rose syrup on the ice.
3. Finish with ½ cup falooda. Stir gently to mix lightly. Serve.

# Rabri

**4 cups full cream milk**
**75 gm khoya - grated, (½ cup)**
**2 tbsp sugar**
**6-8 pistas - chopped**
**3 chhoti illaichi (green cardamoms) - powdered**
**rose petals or silver sheet (varq)**

1. Boil milk in a heavy bottomed kadhai. Add khoya and sugar.
2. Simmer on low-medium heat for about 40-45 minutes, scraping the sides, till the quantity is reduced to almost half and the mixture turns thick with a thick pouring consistency. Remove from fire. The rabri turns thick on keeping.
3. Add some chopped pistas and cardamom powder into the mixture.
4. Transfer to a serving dish and garnish with pistas and rose petals.
5. Chill and serve plain by itself or with jalebis or with some fruit.

# Daribe ki Jalebi

*Picture on page 94*                    *Serves 8*

**1 cup maida, 1 tbsp besan, ¼ tsp (level) soda-bi-carb (mitha soda)**
**½ tbsp melted ghee**
**½ cup thick curd, ghee for frying**
**SYRUP**

**1¼ cups sugar, ¾ cup water, 2-3 pinches orange-red colour**

1. Sieve maida, besan & soda. Add curd & melted ghee. Add ¾ warm water (about ¾ cup) to make a batter of a soft dropping consistency.
2. Beat batter well till smooth. Cover and keep aside for 30-40 minutes.
3. Heat ghee in a frying pan till medium hot. Put the batter in a piping bag and make circles within circle, starting from the outside.
4. Reduce heat. Fry them golden brown on low heat on both sides, turning carefully with a pair of tongs (chimta). Remove from oil, keep aside.
5. For the syrup, boil sugar, water and colour in a kadhai. After the first boil keep on low flame for 5-7 minutes till a stringy syrup is attained.
6. At serving time, dip 4-5 jalebis at a time in the hot syrup for 1 minute, take out and serve them hot with rabri.

# Kale Angoor ki Baraf

*It is somewhat like a chuski. Enjoy it after a spicy chaat session.*

*Makes 6*  *Picture on page 103*

**2 cups black grapes (kale angoor), 2 tbsp powdered sugar, or to taste
½ tsp lemon juice, ½ tsp chaat masala, ½ tsp kala namak (black salt)**

**OTHER INGREDIENTS**
**6 large kulfi moulds, khus syrup, optional**
**6 wooden ice cream spoons or wooden satay sticks (long toothpicks)**
**aluminium foil**

1. Put all ingredients with grapes in a mixer grinder and grind to a smooth puree.
2. Fill each mould only half.
3. Cover the top with aluminium foil. Insert a stick in the foil and place it in the freezer, keeping it upright. Freeze for 3-4 hours or till set.
4. Serve in a small glass, topped with a teaspoon of khus syrup.

# Moong Dal Halwa

*Picture on facing page*                    *Serves 8*

**1 cup dhuli moong dal (skinned green beans)**
**10-12 chhoti illaichi (green cardamoms)**
**1 cup ghee, 2 tsp besan**
**1 cup sugar**
**1 cup milk**
**10-15 almonds - sliced, 10-15 kishmish (raisins)**

1. Soak dal in water overnight or for 8-10 hours. Drain and grind to a fine paste in 2 batches (½ quantity at a time.)
2. Peel cardamoms and powder the seeds and keep aside.
3. Put the skin into a pan with the sugar and add 2 cups water. Stir over medium heat till sugar is dissolved. Simmer for 2 minutes on low heat. Remove from fire and keep aside.
4. Melt ghee in kadhai and fry the besan till lightly brown.

*Contd...*

5. Remove from heat and add the dal paste. (This prevents dal from sticking to the bottom of the kadhai).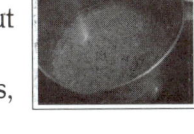

6. Reduce to medium heat and cook stirring, for about 25-30 minutes till golden brown.

7. Add milk a little at a time, stir for about 10-12 minutes, till ghee separates.

8. Stir and cook till golden. When done the fat will begin to separate.

9. Add the almonds and kishmish and cook for 2 minutes.

10. Strain the sugar syrup, add to the mixture and continue to cook and stir till water is absorbed. Bhuno the halwa for about 10 minutes till dry.

11. Sprinkle 2-3 tbsp ghee and cardamom powder. Bhuno on very low heat for 15 minutes till ghee separates and it turns to a rich golden yellow colour. Do not bhuno too much and let it turn brownish and overdone. Serve hot.

◁ *Daribe ki Jalebi : Recipe on page 90*

# Kulfi

*Serves 6*

**1 kg (5 cups) full cream milk, ¼ cup sugar, or to taste, 2 tbsp cornflour
75 gm fresh khoya - grated and mashed (¾ cup)
½ tbsp very finely cut almonds, ½ tbsp pistas - finely sliced
2 drops of kewra essence, seeds of 3-4 chhoti illaichi (green cardamoms)**

1. Dissolve cornflour in 1 cup milk and keep aside.
2. Boil the rest of the milk in a kadhai or deep pan till it is reduced to half the quantity, for about 20 minutes on medium fire.

3. Add sugar and cornflour paste. Cook for 2-3 minutes more till sugar gets dissolved. Remove from fire. Let it cool down a bit.

4. Add khoya, almonds, pista, kewra essence and crushed illaichi.
5. Fill the mixture in kulfi moulds. Freeze for 6-8 hours or overnight.

# Mango Kulfi

*Makes 8*

**1 large mango chopped (1½ cups)**
**6½ cups full cream milk, 7 tbsp sugar**
**seeds of 3-4 chhoti illaichi (green cardamom) - crushed**
**2 tbsp cornflour mixed with ½ cup milk**
**8-10 pistas - blanched & chopped, ½ cup fresh cream**

1. Keeping ½ cup chopped mango aside, puree the rest of the mango (1 cup) with ½ cup milk in a mixer.
2. Boil 6 cups milk with sugar and illaichi for about 20 minutes on low heat till it is reduced to about ½ quantity, about 3 cups.
3. Add cornflour paste stirring continuously. Stir for 5 minutes on low heat. Remove from fire and let the milk cool.
4. Add mango puree to thickened milk. Mix well. Add finely chopped mango pieces and finely chopped pistas also.
5. Add cream. Mix well. Pour into kulfi moulds and freeze for 5-6 hours or overnight.

# Kaju Fruit Rabri

*A wonderful dessert. Serve it in individual mitti ke kasoore (earthernware bowls)
to get the authentic flavour.*

### Serves 8

**1 litre full cream milk**
**¼ cup cashewnuts - powdered coarsely**
**a pinch of mitha soda (soda bi carb)**
**1 tsp lemon juice**
**¼ cup sugar, or to taste**
**seeds of 5-6 chhoti illaichi (green cardamoms) - crushed**

**FRUITS**
**¼ cup green grapes - cut into half**
**¼ cup black grapes - cut into half**
**5-6 orange segments of a small orange - cut into half**
**¼ cup anaar**

**or**

**finely chopped apple with the peel (sprinkle apple pieces with 1 tbsp powdered sugar and a few drops lemon juice to prevent them from turning black)**

1. Boil the milk in a heavy bottomed kadhai. Add powdered cashews and cook on medium low heat, for about 20-25 minutes, till it is reduced to about half the quantity.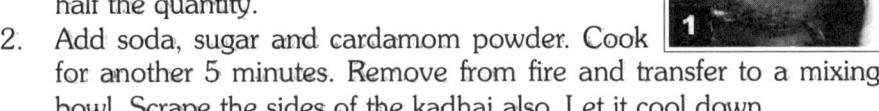
2. Add soda, sugar and cardamom powder. Cook for another 5 minutes. Remove from fire and transfer to a mixing bowl. Scrape the sides of the kadhai also. Let it cool down.
3. Add lemon juice to the cold rabri and beat with a beater.
4. Transfer to individual serving bowls. Keep in the fridge for 15 minutes till the top layer sets a little.
5. Arrange fruits on the top of the rabri. Refrigerate till the time of serving.

# Badaam ki Lauz

*A very special Delhi sweet, which is niether a barfi nor a toffee, but something in between.*

### Makes 16 pieces

**250 gms badaam giri (almonds without hard shell), about 1½ cups**
**½ cup sugar, ¼ cup water**
**varaq (silver leaf)**

1. Put almonds in a bowl. Cover with boiling water. Leave for 15 minutes. Drain and remove skin. Grind blanched almonds coarsely.
2. In a heavy bottom kadhai, put sugar. Pour water on it and stir over low heat till sugar dissolves. Simmer on low heat for 2 minutes.
3. Add almonds and cook stirring continuously for 4-5 minutes, till mixture leaves the sides of the pan.
4. Transfer to a greased thali and level it with greased hands. Decorate with varaq. When cool, cut into squares.

## Hari Chutney

*Serves 6*

½ cup poodina leaves (½ bunch)
1 cup hara dhania (coriander) - chopped along with the stem
2 green chillies - chopped, 2-3 flakes garlic - chopped finely
1 onion - chopped, 1 tbsp lemon juice, or to taste
1½ tsp sugar, ½ tsp salt, a pinch of black salt (kala namak)

1.  Grind all ingredients with just enough water to a smooth paste.

# Saunth (mithi imli chutney)

*Serves 6*

**½ cup seedless imli (tamarind)**
**½ tsp dry ginger powder (sonth)**
**¾ cup gur (jaggery) powder or sugar, to taste**
**½ tsp jeera powder**
**¼ tsp red chilli powder, ¼ tsp garam masala**
**½ tsp saunf powder**
**¼ tsp kalanamak or to taste**

1. Wash imli 2-3 times. Soak imli in 2 cups of water for 10 minutes.
2. Add red chilli powder and bring to a boil, simmer for 2 minutes. Remove from fire and strain. Mash well to extract all the juice.
3. Add all the other ingredients and mix well. Boil. Simmer for 5-7 minutes till thick. Remove from fire and cool. Store in a bottle in the refrigerator.

*Kale Angoor ki Baraf : Recipe on page 91* ⊳

# *Nita Mehta's* BEST SELLERS (Vegetarian)

**CHINESE**
Vegetarian Cuisine

**SANDWICHES**

**Cakes & Chocolates**

**Chutneys, Pickles & Squashes**

**ZERO OIL**

**DAL & ROTI**

**ITALIAN**
Vegetarian Cookery

**Food for Children**

**Soups Salads & Starters**

**MORE SNACKS**

**PANEER** all the way

**QUICK MEALS**